ABANDONED MISSISSIPPI

DESTRUCTION IN THE DEEP SOUTH

JAY FARRELL

AMERICA
THROUGH TIME®
ADDING COLOR TO AMERICAN HISTORY

America Through Time is an imprint of Fonthill Media LLC
www.through-time.com
office@through-time.com

Published by Arcadia Publishing by arrangement with Fonthill Media LLC
For all general information, please contact Arcadia Publishing:
Telephone: 843-853-2070
Fax: 843-853-0044
E-mail: sales@arcadiapublishing.com
For customer service and orders:
Toll-Free 1-888-313-2665

www.arcadiapublishing.com

First published 2019

ISBN 978-1-63499-179-7

Typeset in Trade Gothic 10pt on 15pt
Printed and bound in England

CONTENTS

ABOUT THE AUTHOR

JAY FARRELL is a Nashville, Tennessee, based photographer who loves photographing abandoned structures. He has a passion for utilizing his camera to share the unique, distressed beauty of abandoned homes and structures that most of the world has forgotten. Sharing his adventures with the public through authorship and blogging inspires him as much as the adventures themselves.

INTRODUCTION

The "life after people" feel to abandoned buildings, complete with rotted and caving floors, old contents of yesteryear left behind, and overall entropy and distress are what fuels my inspiration. There's a freedom (and a danger) of hitting the open road and exploring the back road, seeking these abandoned treasures. These structures tell a story. My goal while photographing these them is to tell their stories and be their voice after they've been forgotten, sometimes for generations. Some identify these derelict structures as eyesores or nuisances, others like me see them as art and untold stories.

There is a process to my work. I don't force my way in or vandalize anything, and I don't take or disturb anything. This shows a level of respect and reduces liability. These places are sometimes a hideout for squatters or vandals, which adds potential danger to the situation. It's extremely rare to be confronted by an heir or property owner, but it can happen. The structures are dangerous: roofs caving in, broken glass, nails, needles, wildlife, loose boards, weak floors, etc. You must know what is under your feet. Exploring these structures can be eerie; there are lots of noises, creaks, and constant echoes.

This book features the work from my travels and adventures in Mississippi. I will take you with me on the journey through some of the most dilapidated structures that most people only imagine. You will enjoy an exciting mix of old bygone structures nestled in the woods and cotton fields, defunct churches, a cotton gin, antebellum homes, and so much more.

It's not for the faint of heart, but the walls always tell stories and I enjoy the adventures. In this book, I will make my audience part of the adventure. I take you up close and personal to these tumbling structures, far deeper than the roadside view. You will experience the true feel of rural Mississippi through my lens. I hope you enjoy it!

Take only pictures, leave only footprints. [*Illustration by Kelly J. King*]

1

THE MYSTERY BUILDING

I had only traveled through Mississippi in the past; I never really got to properly explore the state—until now. On a late February morning, I set out for my three-day Mississippi journey, only stopping once in Memphis to enjoy lunch with a friend. All across the South, there were unusual amounts of rainfall during that time, causing flooding in many areas. One could argue that a person of sound mind would not be traveling during times of a natural disaster. However, it was the last day of forecasted rain, and this way, I could get a variety of weather conditions. It was critical to explore before the worst of the overgrowth grew back. Life is about taking risks and capitalizing on opportunities, so off I went.

On my final day in Mississippi, I had plans with a local historian, which will all be revealed later in this book. Besides that, I had no home base or particular direction, except to start in the Northern Mississippi Delta and end up in Northeast Mississippi on my final day, leaving anywhere else as a potential destination. That left a lot of time to explore on instinct, with just me, a camera, and a car. I relied on instinct, patience, and a sense of true north—all of which are important ingredients to successful abandoned photography missions.

The delta region was flat, vast, desolate, and flooded. Very little was stopping the ponding water from rising above the roadways. In many cotton fields, there was enough water for a boat to sail. Wind was high, clouds rolled overhead, and rain was intermittent. DeSoto County was where my first round of exploring began. After navigating through miles of narrow farm community backroads with flooded cotton fields and few houses, I spotted a large abandoned brick building at a deserted crossroads intersection. It was the shape and size of a cotton gin, but there were no other clues besides a few tractor parts and a fire hose hanging up. Everything pointed to the building being a former fire station or county public works building.

Located solely on open land in an area prone to tornadoes, this building stood the test of time that many could not.

The sound of the falling tin beating against the walls was almost rhythmic with the wind.

Right: That's fine handy work, a homemade fan belt rack!

Below: There was this fire hose and more lying across the ground outside the building.

I loved the water dripping off the gear sprocket.

This was likely a former fireplace or wood stove, or maybe for metal working.

The linear view of the inside.

You could say one strong wind could take that flapping tin off the building, but it has withstood many already. Go figure.

2

HOLY WATER

Amid an afternoon of exploring the Northern Mississippi Delta, over and down, one common thread was the many homes dangerously close to flooding. When I made a fuel stop, the man at the store was telling me that many of the older buildings have been claimed by tornadoes or flooding, which explains why quality findings were sparse. But persistence pays off, as always, particularly when getting to know unfamiliar territory. After traveling south a bit, I took a gamble on a backroad heading west, after a tip from a man at that store. He said there was at least one abandoned church, and my adrenaline was rushing with excitement at that point.

Approximately seven miles down that road, traveling through Quitman County, I spotted a lone abandoned church surrounded by woods and field. Drifters or local party crews kicked the door in, so there was easy access for me. Further down that road, there was yet another very old abandoned Missionary Baptist church built on stilts, still sitting in ponding water. These were sad sights, but good fortune for me, as these once proud country churches of the Deep South get their final moment of glory.

Makeshift stained-glass windows were victimized by vandals.

I went through the delta to a church with no name. It was good to get inside and get out of the rain.

Come as you are.

The ladies bathroom had prettier curtains, but they should really restock the paper towels. Or think green and use hand dryers.

This old upright piano has been played on many Sundays, maybe Wednesday nights, too, while the congregations sings hymns.

An old Sunday School room with a vintage heater.

There must have been some piano playing fools in that church to warrant three pianos!

The view of destruction from the pulpit area. The bead board ceiling reveals something important. This church is far older than it looks, and attempts to modernize it with carpet, drop ceiling, etc. covered up beautiful vintage features.

The roof was caved in, but I still wanted to navigate through the marshy ground to see what I could access inside.

It's a holy miracle how this old church still stands at all. Wooden siding entrance, asbestos siding on the sides, all soul.

That was my view from inside the foyer, so I could go no further. The old door on the left was still locked, which was either a bathroom or small office. Forcing it may cause the entire building to fall on me and I'd suffer my eternal fate. Came, conquered, went.

3

SUNNY'S COUNTRY STORE

I knew that I was running out of daylight, so I planned to find "civilization" to do dinner and retire for the night. When driving through a small town called Sledge, Mississippi, I spotted a sign that said "Home Of Charley Pride." I remembered seeing the Grand Ole Opry sign not too long ago, announcing that he was performing there. It's a small world, and the only walls that exist because of distance are ones we put up.

Just before dusk, on a two-lane Panola County, Mississippi, highway, sat a lonely and forgotten country store. Rust and patina was taking over the old metal signage. The old gas pumps and building had not seen employees or customers in years. Many would say the glory days of this store are long over, but I must disagree. Otherwise I would not have stopped. Upon my exit, I passed a house in a small valley that was partially under water, along with several cars submerged to their roofs.

Because every gas station/general store needs a sleeper sofa.

Right: The paint has worn off, and Father Time is taking its rightful spot.

Below: The once active community emporium—home of gas, groceries, and community gossip.

Above: Before the days of pre-pay and credit card swipers at the pumps.

Left: A nicely seasoned kerosene pump with a retro green color nicely completes this stop.

4

THE EASTBOUND MISSISSIPPI HIGHWAY

I stopped in Grenada for the night and got a good night's sleep, despite the hotel room smelling worse than most abandoned houses I visit. Moving right along, getting an early start, the roads were mine to explore. On a two-lane highway headed east and some randomly selected backroad turns, here are some interesting finds along my journey.

My journey continued through both the twisting and straight roads, passing farms, cotton fields, residences here and there, and rural country churches. One common occurrence in Mississippi is that many roads turn into gravel or dirt where county maintenance ends. That often meant I would see nothing, or it was national forest territory. It was all part of the adventure. Sometimes the deeper you go, the more you find—other times not.

This is rare, finding an abandoned restaurant with anything left behind, particularly a small take-out shack. It was randomly placed in the Grenada County countryside, perhaps causing its demise.

I don't think the health inspector would like the kitchen in its current state.

Above: The missing piece of the puzzle. Burger Hut it is.

Right: It's safe to say this overgrown field where this basketball hoop sits used to be a driveway.

The house that owned the field basketball hoop was stuffed to the gills, from every angle.

Because sometimes you just need an old school bus in your yard. Out there, no one will say anything to the contrary. You live your life, let them live theirs.

It's not a matter of having no way in, but more rather nowhere to go, if you do make it in. This took some ingenuity.

This old storefront building caught my eye. Perhaps it was the open storm door and recliner chair in the front. Calhoun County, MS.

There's a clue. Abandoned flower shop.

These do look like old floral design tables. This was alongside the building. Sadly, there was no way in.

5

GRANDPA'S NOT HOME

After passing through Calhoun City, and entering the countryside once again, my next stop was an abandoned cabin sitting a fair distance away from the road. As I approached the cozy old humble abode, I saw that it backed up to woods and a small lake. Undoubtedly, this was someone's dream home at one point. There was a story here that was waiting to be told. I hope you'll follow along and see what seemingly insignificant clues speak to you the most.

A rustic cabin, surrounded by nature, away from everyone. Where do I sign up?

A gutted mattress and an old camp chair. At least the house had air conditioning, even if they make you sleep on that mattress.

Time to test the floors. I didn't fall through, so I suppose they passed the test.

The cabin was slightly larger than it looked from the front angle. What lies ahead on the inside? You're about to see.

I've seen some bizarre and random things in these old houses, but this was the first horse saddle I've seen. The floor through the kitchen was too bad to walk through, so I chose to enter through the front. It pays to be cautious, especially on solo missions like this one.

It's not typical to see clothes and linens still in the closet in abandoned houses. This was a clue.

The remnants of the old electric meter.

It looks like granny's clothes were in the closet, and there were multiple family pictures around the house, most likely of their grandchildren.

An old vintage Hearthglo heater.

A 1980s boom box with cassette player—right on!

The house's decay is making a mess of grandpa's recliner, how rude.

Perhaps there was already a yard sale by the looks of this table. This is getting interesting.

Random litter on the front porch.

This old wooden table had some lovely patina on it, and may have been used for planting/potting.

The living room could use some tidying, but I'm sure I've seen worse.

Sure, scooters belong in the bedroom, why not?

Bathroom is still usable. Don't ask me how I know.

The A-1 Grandpa hat especially is what told the most relevant part of the story for me. Your results may vary.

They had things all ready for when the grandkids visited. Only then, the house probably didn't contain dirt dauber and bird's nests, or decaying, fallen building materials.

This is one of those stops where the house did a great job of storytelling on its own. Now, it has started conceding to nature over the past several years at least. This is the natural order of things, I suppose.

6

THE COTTON GIN

Part of what makes a successful abandoned mission in any specific area or state is capturing locations that speak about what the region is about, including remnants of its past. This old abandoned Chickasaw County cotton gin is part of that past in the Deep South region. I learned the history of this old mill by asking a local at a neighboring store while I was photographing the exterior. He said the mill closed in the 1980s, to the best of his memory.

Cotton gins are used to separate the seeds from the boll of the cotton plant, which saves time over manually separating them. The hulls of the seeds are used for cow feed, and the cottonseed oil, which is extracted from the seed, is used for cooking oil. More modern and efficient means of cotton ginning are available to farmers in present day, and many of these mills have gone by the wayside. Picture this moment in time and envision the sounds of the machinery, workers talking and yelling to each other, and trucks pulling in and out of the mill. The stories the walls can tell are what remain.

A proud part of Mississippi's industrial/agricultural past, in contrast with modern progress.

The inside view on my entrance side. It was an echo chamber inside there. I can still hear the shrill ear-piercing squeal of the tin flapping around, followed by the cracking bang when the loose flaps smacked against the side of the building.

Left: This electrical panel has been long since gutted, internally or by copper scavengers.

Below: Under the front covered porch connecting to a smaller building, and a feed chute used to join the two. Besides, I wasn't trespassing—I was taking photographs.

Many used to call that their cotton gin, and others called it their workplace. This was a spot everyone local knew, back in the day.

I wasn't sure if I could trust that catwalk to get a bird's-eye view, but that didn't mean I didn't attempt it.

A separate room with random contents left behind, or planted by others.

Above left: Those once-moving parts are stuck and rusted in place now.

Above right: This sliding steel door made a horrendous noise when I opened it up a little bit. But my curiosity was satisfied that it did move.

It's hard to say whether this old console television was left behind or if someone treated the vacant building like the town dump. Either way, it was neatly placed.

This was either heating ductwork or a feed chute where the seeds came out.

Above left: This must have been the office, but I was far too late to find anyone there.

Above right: Open office doors are always welcoming. I suppose business hours being posted would be moot at this point.

The inside of the office, which may have been neat and tidy decades ago.

7

GENTRY'S STORE

As I ventured south into Oktibbeha County, after leaving Starkville city limits, I found this magnificent old vintage storefront, formerly Gentry's Store. I knew there was some rich history here that I was eager to uncover. After some research, I was able to get the scoop directly from the source. The Gentry family owns a sigh shop in Starkville, and after confirming it's the same family, I was put in touch with Mr. Buddy Gentry. His father opened the store in 1932, and he grew up in it with his five siblings. Buddy graciously accepted my phone call and shared a lot of community and store history.

The rich history and character of this longtime community staple remains through photographs and memories.

This farming community was tightly knit, and was largely made up of cotton, beef, and dairy cattle farms. This store was a hub and staple of the community where townspeople would trade and socialize. The store sold meats and groceries, dry goods, hardware, animal feed, etc. There was even a gristmill on site that operated before the store was open. Tabs were kept for many families and farms, something common in those days. Buddy told me that Saturday night was the store's busiest time. Buddy's job at closing time on Saturday night was to blink the lights off and on to encourage customers to finalize their purchases. The store's hours were Monday through Saturday, 7 AM - 10 PM, always closed on Sunday.

Cars were invented long before 1932 when the store opened, but many people in the community did not have cars because of finances, or didn't have a need for them yet. Many patrons used horses and wagons for transportation to and from the store, even up until the 1960s. Gentry's Store branched out into selling gas and automotive/farm equipment supplies as time moved on. The store stayed open until approximately 2000, and still sits on family property owned by Buddy's sister. Over the years, farming has declined due to urban growth, housing development, and the younger generation leaving their home bases.

8

WINSTON COUNTY WRECKAGE

After leaving the Starkville/Oktoc area, I traveled south for what seemed like an age. I just wanted to experience as much as possible while really getting a feel for the lay of the land. The road gets lonely, but there's also a freedom associated with exploring. I've been asked why I wouldn't bring someone along for these longer multi-day excursions. The answer is simple: scheduling conflicts, and I can't have anyone with me who is antsy or nagging. This game takes patience, and sometimes you put in far more than you get out. That, however, is a matter of perspective. Not every abandoned building or house makes the cut either. Less is more, when I find places that resonate with me.

Following a lull period, I turned off the two-lane highway onto a backroad, where I saw an old abandoned house sitting on the corner, perched on a small hilltop. I was in Winston County, Central Mississippi at this point in my journey. First I explored farther down that road so I could finish at the corner, closest to my exit. This road was promising. Sadly, it was short. I did stop at one crumbling house in the woods, and then went back to the house on the corner. Photo captions will narrate the remainder of this segment.

My first thought, was this place too abandoned? As bad as it looks, there was still something waiting for me inside.

Times were hard financially, apparently. Plywood cabinet doors are not the norm, but certainly resourceful. It's even harder to imagine someone paying for that green paint. I hope it was on clearance.

This is not your typical indoor plumbing—these favor outdoor water spigots. Very interesting.

I'm surprised I was even able to navigate through the home's interior by the first look of the outside.

Left: No one is around to use the ladder. But the birds and dirt daubers aren't afraid to.

Below: This front porch was one area I could not walk on.

The trees surrounding the house probably protected it all these years. This is what decades of abandonment looks like.

An old International truck buried in the weeds and trees at the next house.

This guy's record keeping skills were on par for sure.

Possibly ransacked by someone, but pretty much left as it was, I'd bet.

This is the only angle I could photograph this house from. The overgrowth in the front was too thick for me to get a clean shot. I suppose Mississippi overgrowth doesn't care as much that it was still winter.

The contents inside the carport behind the house.

The old box fan is still plugged in, and family pictures are still where they were left. This is eerie on some level.

We know this person was religious and interested in gardening. The calendar on the wall was dated 2013, which seems accurate based on the state of the home. Elements, temperature, humidity, and not being occupied will take its toll on a building.

Pull up a seat, stay a while.

The old screen door has fallen, now gently touched by the light.

9

CHOCTAW COUNTY

At the conclusion of my stops in Winston County, I continued west with my destination unknown. At a crossroads several miles ahead, I made a turn onto a southbound backroad, which took me into Attala County. After a series of backroads and one seemingly never-ending dirt and gravel road, I decided to continue elsewhere before going back to Northeast Mississippi, where I needed to be the next day. Not far into that part of my travels, I passed a no frills road sign that said "Entering Choctaw County." Soon after that, I saw these distressed, antique Detroit steel gems that I knew I had to stop for.

My next stop was in a small charming town called Sturgis. I almost missed this adorable old house nestled in a valley on a residential side street. In certain cases, my peripheral vision set off false alarms, but this was a solid lead.

On the way to Aberdeen, where I planned to settle for the night, I saw this small country cottage that was missing the front exterior walls. Upon closer examination, I saw it was due to a fire. This was a bizarre enough sighting to require a stop.

Circa 1948 Chevrolet, according to my research.

Many people are great at starting projects like this—not many finish them.

Circa 1948 Chevy truck. This would be something to go through mechanical and just drive it like it is. So much character and patina, I hope it drives again.

Interior view of a duplicate Chevrolet sedan.

This charming old house sits by itself and is left behind with nothing else like it on that road.

The back of the house.

Left: This 1950s metal porch chair is full of character and patina, a salvage store's dream.

Below: The tree looks like it's growing into this gutted mattress. Neither side is giving an inch.

I entered through the front door, despite neighbors possibly seeing me. The floor was too rotted at the back entrance. This was questionable too, but it paid off.

More hanging clothes. I see a pattern. This wallpaper and the house itself were probably products from the early 1900s.

I think the newest items and furnishings I found inside this house were from the 1980s, which gives a rough timeline of the house's abandonment.

That's one way to do a bunk bed. My only hope was that if the floors were strong enough to hold all that clutter, I would be okay if I walked softly.

Usually this clear a view of a bathroom requires getting inside.

I didn't even have to go inside to get inside. The tiny cottage was in questionable condition before the fire damage occurred, or so it seems.

The little house looks like a barn with windows from that angle.

The lone chimney no longer connected to the house was the first bizarre thing that caught my eye. This was an entertaining quick stop.

10

THE HISTORIAN

This is a special treat, and a *tour de force* that I was able to put together for the first time. The historian in Lamar County, Alabama, who gave me history information on a Victorian mansion I photographed there, referred me to a Mississippi historian she knew. When I contacted Mrs. Jerry Harlow with the Monroe County Mississippi Historical Society, she eagerly agreed to be a ride-along for some exploring, and she would show me some local Monroe County, Northeast Mississippi historical locations. This is a huge honor and an experience I enjoyed, so let's begin the journey. On the way to pick Jerry up, I found an old gas station and an abandoned house in Aberdeen near her house.

I get that this was a full-service gas station, but does anyone else find this sign a bit nonsensical?

Left: Please, sell more wiper blades! Maybe drivers would be less stupid in the rain. I'm not betting on it though. Too bad this place isn't selling them any longer.

Below: The famous gas station restrooms.

Someone got mad when the soap ran out.

This was a rather creepy shell of a house. There were no steps to access the raised level old house, but I was happy to get this.

Above: This *circa* 1968 Ford pickup truck had some remarkable character, slowly being claimed by nature.

Left: After picking Jerry up, this was one of the first places we stopped. This is an old oil pump at a defunct oil distribution office.

Contrasting lines and textures are always interesting at old industrial buildings.

I always think of the customers and employees who depended on these now abandoned commercial buildings.

Circa 1853 antebellum mansion, raised cottage style. Sadly it's boarded up and there's no inside access, but this is a great representation of a Mississippi antebellum house.

Above left: This house has been abandoned for decades, but at one time, an engineering professor attempted to do some renovation with some students. But these boards are as far as they got.

Above right: One of the brilliant features, the two-level porch.

Above left: The back of the house, in similar levels of disrepair.

Above right: This steel staircase is reminiscent of ones used in industrial applications.

I couldn't resist doing a romantic sun flare accentuating the features of this antebellum wonder.

Left: Antique water meter in front of the former site of the large cotton compress that used to serve the area.

Below: One of two walls, and a slab remaining of the old cotton compress plant that served Aberdeen, Prairie, and surrounding areas. Its demise was caused by a fire in one of the buildings, decreased cotton production, and newer technology for compressing cotton.

This smokestack is one of the few remains of the old Gulf Ordnance Plant in Prairie, MS, that manufactured bombs before and during World War II. When the war started, men were soldiers, and more women worked the plant to make bombs. Firewalls were installed to help prevent damage to other areas in the event of an accidental explosion.

There was access to this stack by driving down a dirt road, and walking across marshy grass and prairie dirt that required careful footing. Workers lived in dormitories on the plant property. Higher paid supervisors had larger houses than general workers. The oppressive side of capitalism was alive and well.

Left: They probably removed lower hooks to save some people from their own bad judgment, thinking of climbing it.

Below: This was the only other original building left. Sadly there were piles of stinky manure, marshland, and a pond blocking my access. Jerry also told me that after the war, the facility became a vocational school for soldiers returning from war.

This is an original slave cabin still standing, on the grounds of the former Holiday-Evans plantation in Prairie, circa 1850. The plantation was miles long in its day.

Well built, yet still as rustic and primal as it gets. Many plantations folded after slavery was abolished and sharecropping ended. Overall, how plantations operated changed. Some advanced, while others stayed behind and withered away.

This period of American history, and what these cabins stood for, is disturbing. As one of the few left of its kind, the building that still stands is history at its finest and richest.

Historic Old Athens Jail, built in 1845 by architect Joshua Toomer. He was incidentally incarcerated there himself after a bit of alcohol-related celebration and taking the wrong horse. The jailer's living quarters were downstairs. The upstairs housed the jail cells where prisoners' shackles were fastened to the floor. The historical society has started and will continue renovation.

11

FROZEN IN TIME

This magnificent antebellum-era house was the final stop that Mrs. Jerry, the historian, brought me to. Not only does this fine work of art need its own chapter, but we saved the best for last with this particular stop. The grand old house sat on a hill over 100 feet back from the road, after climbing six crumbling concrete stairs from the road shoulder. There was a surprisingly thick concentration of overgrowth, especially considering itv was still winter. Jerry knew this place would be right up my alley, but wisely decided to wait in the car while I risked falling through the floors and getting scratched up by thorn bushes. Whatever could have happened, it may have very well been worth it.

The cleanest photograph I could get of the front side of the old antebellum house, built in the 1860s-1870s, according to history records Jerry dug up.

The door was boarded shut and this front screened-in porch had extremely bad floors and joists. I knew this was not my way inside. Those tires seemed randomly placed, but I was not expecting the surprise I was about to discover as I made my way around the side of the house.

This is the only view I could get of the front porch. It looks quite hospitable with the porch swing.

Texture, shape, and wild brush, as I navigated through vegetation and thorn bushes to access the side and back.

This circa 1957 Ford ragtop was certainly unexpected—but wait, there is more. LOTS more.

The layers of oxidation and paint make an interesting texture, but it's sad to see such a classic sink into the ground and rot away.

Another Detroit gem, among many others behind the house. It was like a miniature antique car graveyard! The thick vegetation and marshy ground made it difficult for me to access all of them, but rest assured, I'm bringing you the goods.

An old Enterprise gas stove and Kenmore washing machine, common backyard ornaments at abandoned houses in these parts.

This is a good vantage point showing multiple antique cars that have sat there for decades.

Left: The back view of the house. There were so many things capturing my attention, I couldn't decide where to start. The moment of truth needed to be revealed. Was there a way in the house?

Below: This interesting basin was mounted to the wall right at the entry point through the back door, as I entered the kitchen.

This kitchen table probably had more carburetors sitting on top of it than people eating off of it.

How many refrigerators does one house need? There was a third one in the next room.

Above: I don't want to accuse anyone of being a hoarder, but someone was.

Left: It's a wonder that these very old clothes haven't been completely eaten by moths. This was a clue.

True to my word, the third refrigerator.

Me photographing their Kodacolor package—how life circles around.

Above: I'm as tough as they come when it comes to not being spooked, but I must admit, this living room was a bit eerie. The temperature dropped the farther I went into the house.

Left: Do I dare go up these steps? Of course! They were solid, as was most of the upstairs floor.

Before going upstairs, I wanted to complete the first floor. This was one of the bedrooms, complete with a fireplace.

Here was the other downstairs bedroom. The crib seems out of place—you will know why later.

One of the upstairs rooms.

And another. I did not go in because in the far corner, a good chunk of the floor was rotted away, probably due to a roof leak. With 12-foot-tall ceilings, it would not have been a pleasant fall.

I still can't believe how much literature was all over the floors. There were magazines and newspapers, too many to look through. I noticed dates from the 1960s through the mid 1980s. That, and the age of the appliances, provided a rough timeline for how long this house had been abandoned.

The opposite view of the kitchen on my way out.

This house did a great job telling its own story for the most part. This whole experience was exactly like stepping into a retro time capsule. As I would interpret this, the former occupants were elderly and passed on, and the house has just been sitting. Either there were no heirs, or the heirs just haven't done anything. I wasn't far off, but it was nice to get more local intel.

Jerry was able to give me a bit of history that she knew about the house and past residents, which is even better. The last occupants of the once-proud antebellum home were two maiden sisters. The only known heir was their nephew, who stored the old cars there. By then, the sisters were probably very elderly and didn't meet him with much resistance. She believes they passed away some time in the 1980s, and did not know if the nephew was still alive. He probably had all kinds of aspirations to fix up those old cars. But the result you've seen is the typical result when someone says they will do that. I'm glad I was able to tell this forgotten story.

12

THE UNEXPECTED BONUS

Following a very enjoyable (and educational) outing with Mrs. Jerry, I was excited about the days I spent exploring and photographing abandoned Mississippi, and started my journey home. Approximately twenty-five minutes of backroad travel landed me in Western Alabama, which was my most direct route home. At that point, I was buzzing about my trip, and was not actively looking for other abandoned locations. I was also eager to get home, and it would take an impressive find for me to stop. Well, that happened. Twice. Sometimes it works out that way, but who's complaining?

First, I saw a small, very old rural church sitting alone on a slight hillside, approximately fifteen minutes outside of town, appearing to be abandoned for several years at least. I later reached out to Jerry and asked her if she recognized it. She thought it was the former "Grubtoe Church," which was renamed later. Research was tricky because of name changes and many other churches disappearing. If it's the church I think, it was built in 1922 and later became a Free Will Baptist church.

Jerry said that over the years, rural churches have declined in number, and have been struggling. More of the younger generations, with new families, attend churches in town, because there are more programs for them and their kids. Slightly larger churches tend to be more forward thinking in their approach to worship, social activities, and other programs. If the smaller rural churches don't evolve, and their older congregation gradually dies off, that leaves them with an uncertain future. It takes resources for any church or business to operate. All else aside, I love old church buildings.

Once I got back on course, I only got a quarter-mile down the road, and what happened? I saw an old crumbling abandoned roadside cabin nestled in the woods. There was no driveway or neighboring houses. The only sign of civilization was a tractor path on farm property behind the cabin. I hope you enjoy these unexpected bonus stops, and most of all, my adventures in Mississippi.

This charming Deep South country church has seen multiple generations and hopes for a rescue one day.

I'd wager that air conditioner worked overtime on those hot sticky Mississippi summer days.

There was no way in from either side, and the back steps were rotted. I was still happy I stopped.

No exaggeration, it really is a cabin in the woods, as authentic as it gets.

Above: There wasn't much inside. It was very primal. I saw no sign of previous electric service.

Left: Someone cared enough to lock it, even though part of the back is wide open.

Warm sun and ghostly shadows from the trees create a nice compliment to the distressed structure.

These chairs blocked the back entry, which was a good disclaimer, because that floor was very weak.

MORE BY JAY FARRELL

ABANDONED ALABAMA
VOLUME 1
ISBN: 978-1-63499-114-8

ABANDONED ALABAMA
VOLUME 2
ISBN: 978-1-63499-161-2

ABANDONED KENTUCKY
VOLUME 1
ISBN: 978-1-63499-056-1

ABANDONED NASHVILLE
ISBN: 978-1-63499-113-1

ABANDONED TENNESSEE
VOLUME 1
ISBN: 978-1-63499-055-4

ABANDONED TENNESSEE
VOLUME 2
ISBN: 978-1-63499-102-5